IMAGES
of England

DONCASTER
1950s-1960s

A scene on Doncaster railway station on the occasion of the Plant Centenary with A4 60014 *Silver Link*.

IMAGES
of England

DONCASTER
1950s-1960s

Peter Tuffrey

TEMPUS

First published 2002
Copyright © Peter Tuffrey, 2002

Tempus Publishing Limited
The Mill, Brimscombe Port,
Stroud, Gloucestershire, GL5 2QG

ISBN 0 7524 2612 5

Typesetting and origination by
Tempus Publishing Limited
Printed in Great Britain by
Midway Colour Print, Wiltshire

A view of Market Place near the junction with High Fisher Gate.

Contents

Acknowledgements

I would like to thank the following people who have been most helpful in the production of this book: Eric Braim, Doug Brown, Ken Elliff, Geoff Elvin, Ray Nortrop, Hugh Parkin and Charlie Worsdale.

Carr House Road looking west before the properties on the left were demolished for the construction of the southern relief road.

Introduction

I suppose everyone has a period in their lives which they enjoyed most or found most exciting, and I must admit that the late 1950s and 1960s are particularly favourite periods of mine. It was a time when we emerged from the austerity of the post-war years with rationing, unemployment and poor housing and a time of the Beat Boom where attitudes changed. But most of all the 1950s and '60s were times when many Local Authorities put into action their plans for the re-development of their roads, housing, shopping centres and light industrial sites. Doncaster was no exception to this and in fact probably underwent as much upheaval during the late 1950s and '60s as at any time during its long history. Before the town's development plan was put into operation everything in the town centre was mixed up together. People were living in poor housing conditions alongside congested roads, light industrial sites and commercial areas. So there was a total re-organization of the town centre and some would argue it was long overdue. Being born in 1953 I saw most of this new work being undertaken. Entire streets were cleared and new houses and shopping centres were built. But whilst I was still a young boy, I did not fully appreciate what precisely was going on at the time and this in some way has attracted me to produce this book. I have gathered pictures and information about the main activities being undertaken and now feel more enlightened. In turn I hope that when people read through this book they will gain an understanding about how important a period the 1950s and '60s were to the town's development.

I think it is particularly fascinating to examine some of the aerial pictures taken in 1951 to see how the town looked just before much of the work took place. It is almost like a final glimpse at the town before it had its make-over. Once the demolition work got underway it is amazing to see vast areas of wide open spaces in the St James and Cleveland Street areas before the high rise flats were erected.

Some people will have fond memories when seeing the old shops, now long gone, that they once frequented in the town centre. I still have get a twinge of nostalgia when looking at the pictures of Cuttriss's model shop on Cleveland Street where boys used to spend hours of their time on most Saturdays. Others, perhaps a little older than myself, will have happy if not blurred memories recalling times they spent in the pubs that were swept away in the name of progress.

Whilst I was not old enough to be able to see many of the top pop groups appear in the town, largely at the Gaumont Cinema (now Odeon) I'm pleased, thanks to local press photographer Charlie Worsdale, to include pictures of the various acts in here. Most of the other pictures have been taken from a variety of sources.

Some may argue that a book containing pictures and information from the 1950s and 60s is too premature but I don't think it is, particularly when looking at a town like Doncaster. It shows how things have changed in such a relatively short space of time and allows us to judge if things have changed for the better. If they haven't we can make a reassessment and put things right, if indeed they are wrong, once the opportunity arises.

Balloon seller at the Cleveland Street/Baker Street corner.

One
Rambling Round

The High Street/Baxter Gate junction during the trolley bus era. Vehicles travelled along Baxter Gate whilst on the Beckett Road/Wheatley Hills routes.

A busy scene in Baxter Gate looking towards the Market Place. Featured on the right are the business premises of Freeman, Hardy and Willis with the Blue Bell public house just beyond. On the left Woolworths, Owen Owen and Beetham's public house can be seen. Early in October 1950, news came that the Liverpool firm of Owen Owen Ltd had bought the store of Verity & Sons Ltd, Baxter Gate. Owen Owen had branches at Liverpool, Preston, Blackpool, and Coventry. The business was to continue under the existing management until control finally passed to Owen Owen who dealt in similar kinds of goods to Verity's.

Another view of Baxter Gate, a little closer to Clock Corner, with the Market Place in the distance.

The Elmfield Café, on the east side of Bennetthorpe, taken from near the war memorial. The café has since been converted to a private dwelling. The derivation of the name Bennetthorpe is said to be attributable to Joseph Bennett who once lived in the area.

Bennetthorpe looking towards the town centre. All the buildings up to the Rockingham Arms Hotel have since been demolished. The pub was erected in 1778 and rebuilt around 1923 to the designs of Allen & Hickson.

Bowers Fold looking from the Market Place through to Silver Street; the Stamp Corner is on the right. The properties on that side were cleared and the site redeveloped around the mid-1960s. The Stamp Corner was subsequently housed in the new development. Jim Webb established the business in the late 1940s.

Bridge Terrace with the Railway (Plant) Works in the distance and a lorry belonging to Heath and Smith in left foreground. The street name was obviously derived from the close proximity of the seven-arched St James' Bridge built in 1852. Bridge Terrace, built during the latter half of the nineteenth century, was demolished as a result of a compulsory purchase order during the late 1950s. A number of the residents were rehoused in purpose-built flats at Wheatley.

Cartwright Street facing Waterdale. House building began there during the early nineteenth century and was slow, spanning a considerable period. Note the balconies on some of the properties in the top picture. The thoroughfare was demolished during the 1960s under the Central Area Number 3 compulsory purchase order. The old route of the street is the one that now extends through the Waterdale shopping precinct between Cleveland Street and Waterdale.

House clearance in Baker Street.

This section of Carr House Road once stretched between Cemetery Road and Bentinck Street – seen in the distance on the right. All the properties have since been cleared.

This picture was taken near the southern end of Cemetery Road looking along Carr House Road. The Hyde Park (Corporation) Schools are on the right with Arthur Street and the Prince of Wales public house just beyond. The Hyde Park Schools, designed by the Borough Surveyor, were opened by the mayor on 26 September 1895, for 220 boys, 220 girls and 272 mixed infants. Today the school is the only survivor from this scene.

Cleveland Street at the junction with Portland Place featuring H. Brown's Television and Radio Exchange business premises at No. 102. One of the signs on his building states: 'Trouble free R.G.D. Try Me.' The Assemblies of God Pentecostal church may be seen on the extreme right. Cleveland Street, named after the Duke of Cleveland, was opened as a thoroughfare in 1833-34. The extensive demolition work, which took place along the street during the 1960s, was spread over several compulsory purchase orders.

A splendid view of a Doncaster fire engine speeding along Cleveland Street in the early 1960s. The junction with Baker Street is immediately behind the vehicle. A new fire station in Lonsdale Avenue was opened on 10 March 1937 and included five flats for five full-time firemen.

Two views of Clock Corner which was constructed during 1895, replacing an earlier edifice dating from 1838. The new Clock Corner was built as part of the widening of Baxter gate and was designed by J.G. Walker. The Mayoress Mrs F. Brightmore in the presence of the Corporation and a crowd of the general public started the clock at noon on 13 February 1895.

East Laith Gate with Sunny Bar in the distance. The license of the King's Head public house on the left, dating from at least the 1790s, was transferred to new premises in the Bradford Row precinct during November 1965. The old premises, which had been rebuilt during the course of their history, were subsequently demolished. Past owners of the pub included Margaret Walker, Hewitt Bros and Hammond United Breweries Ltd.

The west side of French Gate before it was cleared for the construction of the Arndale (now French Gate) Centre. The buildings featured include the Bay Horse public house and Greenhills Ltd (drapers), converted from the Electra/Regal cinema; it is seen here after it was turned into a shop. Jays Furnishing stores at Nos 55-57 is on the right. During mid-December 1957 it was reported that the Regal, formerly the Electra, in French Gate was to close at the end of the month. At the time, the cinema was running at a loss of £10 a week. It was built in 1911 and had 500 seats.

Much adverse comment was made when the Guildhall, French Gate, dating from 1848, was demolished. Many people argued that such a splendid façade fashioned in the Classical style should have been retained and incorporated into the new Marks & Spencer development. Once housed in the Guildhall were the Law Courts and the Police headquarters with a number of cells for offenders.

The west side of French Gate facing the North Bridge, *c.* 1963. The buildings include those occupied by John Collier (tailor), S. Green (gowns), the Angel & Royal Hotel, Wine Shop and the Famous Army Stores Ltd. Queen Victoria and the Prince Consort visited the inn during 1851. Another famous visitor was Charles Dickens, the novelist, in 1857.

A panoramic view of French Gate. Several buildings on the left up to the White Swan public house were cleared for the construction of the east by-pass. Amongst these were Ye Olde Barrel Snack Bar, Electrical Wholesalers Ltd, Denbighs (cleaners) and Jacksons. Ye Olde Barrel Café was formerly known as the Golden Barrel dating back to at least 1822, though the licence lapsed during January 1937.

The French Gate/Lord Street junction with the Weights and Measures Office on the left. Trolley buses used the route, seen here, whilst travelling to and from the Grey Friars Road depot.

Another view showing Ye Olde Barrel Cafe and that demolition work has started in Frenchgate for the construction of the east by-pass.

Catherine Street looking towards Carr House Road. Houses were built on Catherine Street in small numbers from around 1866 by local builders. Gill Street, a short thoroughfare, once linking Jarratt Street and Catherine Street, is still in existence but truncated at the former Catherine Street end.

The junction of Green Dyke Lane and Cemetery Road with the Old Cemetery and Carr Lane to the left. Much controversy was caused during the 1970s when the houses on Green Dyke Lane (in the distance on the right), mainly built during the latter half of the nineteenth century, were demolished for the construction of the Southern Relief Road.

Local botanist and horticulturist Samuel Appleby, writing in 1866, said that Green Dyke Lane, seen here from Cemetery Road looking west, took its name from a wide stagnant ditch. This ran from the Carr Lane corner to St James' pond, near the site of the old Shakespeare's Head public house. The cemetery on the left was opened on 1 January 1856, with a chapel following a design by Sir Gilbert Scott, and was extended in 1882.

Church view looking north taken by local photographer Geoff Warnes on 4 December 1954. On the left is the old tram/trolley bus depot, which was opened on 2 June 1902 and demolished during the 1980s. On the right is the Technical School.

Marsh Gate and a fine array of buses with the Bridge Hotel on the left, another view taken by Geoff Warnes. In the distance on the right is Saint Andrews church.

The top of Hall Gate with Cooplands on the left and the Gaumont (now Odeon on the right). The films showing at the time the picture was taken were *London in the Raw and The Big Risk*. The Gaumont was opened on 3 September 1934 and renamed the Odeon on 20 January 1987. Cooplands can trace their history back to 1931 when the business was established by Alice Coopland (later Jenkinson).

A panoramic view of Hall Gate, once part of the Great North Road. Featured on the right is the Art Deco frontage of the Ritz cinema and the business premises of house furnishers Postlethwaite & Stacey. Meller's Dolls Hospital can be identified on the left. The Ritz cinema officially opened on 26 November 1934. It was renamed the Odeon in 1955 and closed on 7 July 1973.

The east side of Hall Gate seen before the buildings at the centre of the picture were demolished for the Bradford Row precinct.

Another view of the east side of Hall Gate. James Frederick Monks, whose business premises are illustrated here, had been a Doncaster printer for many years and died in Middlewood Hospital, Sheffield, in July 1957 at the age of seventy-nine. Founder of the firm of J.F. Monks (Doncaster) Ltd, J. Monks had been in business as a printer in Doncaster since the 1890s. He came to Doncaster from Bradford to set up as a printer in Scot Lane, forming the printing business of Wilson & Monks. From Doncaster he went to Margate where he established the Electric Press and remained there until 1914 when he moved to London to become an overseer in a London works. After the First World War he returned to Doncaster to establish the business of J.F. Monks which was subsequently carried on by his son Walter B. Monks.

The High Street/Hall Gate junction with Silver Street to the left. The Prudential Chambers building off centre to the left was erected in 1912 to the designs of Paul Waterhouse, an ex-president of the Royal Institute of Architects. The White Bear Hotel adjacent to the right underwent extensive alterations in 1959.

High Fisher Gate, off Market Place, with Sunny Bar in the distance. P. Platts & Sons business premises may be seen on the right. Thomas Yates founded the business of J.C. & T. Yates, agricultural engineers, around 1862, and it eventually passed to his two sons. Bernard Fowler Yates, the last surviving partner, sold the business in 1941 to Messrs P. Platts. The company dealt with agricultural machinery.

These two pictures show a section of High Street featuring Kendalls, the Picture House, the Stylo and Milns & Co. Towards the end of March 1933, it was announced that Messrs Millns & Co., the cycle agents and dealers, and wireless experts, were transferring their business to another part of town. For the previous twenty years the firm had been closely identified with the business life of St Sepulchre Gate, where they had carried on a flourishing and rapidly extending trade, first at No. 165, and later at 92-94. The firm moved to more commodious and more central premises at No. 9 High Street, two doors away from the Picture House. The new premises, which had undergone extensive alterations, provided ample accommodation for a big display of cycles, motorcycles, wireless sets, gramophones and all the accessories incidental to that business. The reconstructed premises formed an arcade, with a large increase in window space, in which stock-in-trade was displayed to the best advantage. Millns & Co moved from High Street during the 1960s.

High Street facing north, the business premises featured on the right include those belonging to Mac Fisheries Ltd, J. & G. Oldfield, the Outsize Shop (Greville & Stuart, gowns and costumes), Atkinson's Tobacco Stores and the Eagle Star Insurance Co. Ltd.

High Street facing north, with the Danum Hotel and Mansion House to the left.

High Street facing Hall Gate where the premises of J. G. Timmins and Wild & Sykes may be seen on the left. Perhaps more than any other trade, the tobacconist depends on casual custom, rather than a regular family business. So, to the credit of J.G. Timmins & Co. – Tobacconists and Gentlemen's Hairdressers, formerly at No. 22 High Street and Sunny Bar – it was claimed that most of their customers were 'regular' callers. The firm had been studying the requirements of smokers from around 1906, and developed a standard of promptness and courtesy. As well as carrying all the standard brands of cigarettes, cigars and smoking mixtures, Timmins' blended a mixture of their own which made quite a name for itself. Their 'Kentucky' tobacco was a pure Virginia which found a ready welcome in the pipes of discriminating smokers. A wide range of smokers' accessories, including pipes, cigarette cases, holders, tobacco pouches, lighters, tobacco jars, fancy match boxes, etc., were always displayed at both shops. And it was once said: 'For those perplexed relatives who cannot think of a gift for confirmed smokers, the problem is satisfactorily solved here.'

The Gentlemen's Toilet Saloons were alleged to have been among the finest equipped in the district, rivalling any others in both surroundings and service. And 'expert' hairdressers were employed who were courteous and efficient, and above all 'never obtrusive.'

Even in 1958, at the ripe old age of eighty-two, William Wild, of Balmoral Road Doncaster, still maintained an active interest in the firm of Wild & Sykes, High Street, Doncaster, the firm of which he was the joint founder some fifty years earlier. He came to Doncaster from the Wakefield area, where he worked in a colliery supplies store, and established a similar business in partnership with H. Sykes. He was the head of three generations of the Wild family, who were then associated with the firm. His son Stanley was a partner, and Stanley's son Peter also worked there. W. Wild and his original partner pioneered the colliery supply trade in the Doncaster area. It was said he had seen many changes in the district and had watched the gradual development of the town into an important mining centre.

View from the North Bridge glancing towards Marsh Gate where (Jack) Temple's Model Lodging House and the Bridge Hotel may be seen on the left. A large sign in the centre of the picture advertises the products of the Manor Hardware Co. Ltd in Marsh Gate. The Bridge Hotel, built around 1912, replaced the 'Labour in Vain' which was demolished for the construction of the North Bridge. The pub survived until around 1972.

North Bridge with the town centre in the distance and the Brown Cow public house on the immediate right. The pub was rebuilt around 1908 to accommodate the construction of the Bridge. *The Doncaster Chronicle* of 18 July 1963 stated, 'Terms of compensation have been provisionally agreed for the Brown Cow Inn, North Bridge Road, Doncaster, which the [Doncaster] Corporation require in connection with the proposed North Bus Station. The District Valuer has reported to the Planning Committee on the terms provisionally agreed with the owners Samuel Smiths.' The *Yorkshire Evening Post* of 27 August 1964 carried a picture of the Brown Cow being demolished in 1964.

Another view from North Bridge where French Gate and North Bridge Road merged. The chemist's shop on the right belonging to C.R. Ford Ltd was No. 1 North Bridge Road. Trafford Street (on the right) also joined with the two thoroughfares here. Confectioners S. Travis Ltd were at Nos 3-5 North Bridge Road and one of their vans may be seen.

View from Lord Street of the backs of houses on Church View. St George's church may be seen in the distance. All the houses were cleared by the late 1980s.

Another view from Lord Street but this time showing houses on Cheswold Road, named after the river which once flowed nearby. The houses were cleared by the late 1980s.

View along St Sepulchre Gate with Jacob's Corner in the distance.

Harry Jacobs' building is on the right and Boddy's shop is in the centre of this view. During February 1953 D.L. Staniland & Co. sold drapers Boddy Bros' premises, at the Duke Street/St Sepulchre Gate corner, to H. Samuel Ltd, jewellers of Rockley, Birmingham. The firm of Boddy Bros was started in 1879 in a small shop at No. 68 St Sepulchre Gate by J. W. Boddy and originally traded in fancy goods. The firm prospered from the start and in 1888 acquired No. 60 St Sepulchre Gate where a gentleman's outfitters was established. J.W. Boddy's three sons Percy, Herbert and J.W. (Jnr) were all brought up in the business. In 1896 J.W. Jnr opened a further branch in the Market Place, but that was closed down in December 1950, and the firm concentrated on the St Sepulchre Gate premises. Earlier, in 1923, the shop at the Duke Street/St Sepulchre Gate corner was rebuilt. The business premises were disposed of in 1953 due to the retirement of the partners.

St Sepulchre Gate at the junction with Elsworth Street. All the properties, mainly built during the latter half of the nineteenth century, were cleared by the late 1960s.

Commercial and business premises on St Sepulchre Gate. Most of these we cleared during the mid-1960s to facilitate the construction of the Inner Relief Road. For many years the Victoria Rooms were associated with the Bullars family. Note that the Clydesdale Supply Co. Ltd's premises have already been vacated, as have those formerly occupied by gents' hairdresser, C.E. Wheeler. Jeweller S. Gordon is announcing a closing down sale and that 'everything must be cleared'.

Both pictures show properties on the southern side of St Sepulchre Gate awaiting demolition for the construction of the Arndale (now French Gate) Centre. 'Doncaster is said to have lost its soul, but it has certainly gained a new heart.' So said the town's mayor Alderman Mrs Elsie Stenson during January 1968, when describing her impressions of the new £3 million Arndale Developments Ltd shopping centre which was expected to be opened in May. Along with other members of the town council and officials of the Doncaster Corporation, the mayor had been invited to a preview visit to the centre. S.H. Chippindale, managing director of Arndale Development Ltd accompanied the civic party on their tour and later he said that he hoped to submit, in March, detailed plans for the second phase of the development. These plans would provide for the further extension of the Centre westwards over Factory Lane to Station Road, and would include another two large multiple units to 'balance' the two British Home Stores and Boots. In the current phase Hodgson & Hepworth Ltd would be housed in one of these redeveloped multiple units and they were in negotiations with one of the very large women's fashions multiples for the other.

St Sepulchre Gate, with the Leopard Hotel on the left, showing some of the properties eventually demolished for the construction of the Inner Relief Road.

A final flurry of business is seen here on St Sepulchre Gate before the premises fell victim to the demolition hammer in order for the Arndale Shopping Centre to be built.

St Sepulchre Gate featuring the Elephant Hotel and the business premises of Manfields. During early March 1975, it was announced that the Elephant Hotel, St Sepulchre Gate, which had closed in the previous year, was likely to be demolished. At a meeting of the DMBC technical services committee, outline planning permission for the demolition and the redevelopment of the site as a three-storey branch bank was given to the Yorkshire Bank Ltd.

Premises awaiting demolition on St Sepulchre Gate due to the Inner Relief Road redevelopment scheme. W. Poynter left his home in the snow on Monday 24 February 1958 to buy some cigarettes from a Beckett Road shop, but later he was found dead near a garage at the rear of Avenue Road, a short distance from his home. His body was discovered by another businessman, Ernest Hill, grocer and provision merchant of Beckett Road. E. Hill said: 'I went to him to see what I could do but he was beyond help and I telephoned for the police and an ambulance'. William Fielding Poynter (sixty), was a single man and proprietor of W. Poynter & Son, beef and pork butchers of St Sepulchre Gate, Doncaster, a business established by his grandfather W. Poynter a century earlier. In his will published during November of that year, W.F. Poynter did not forget his friends in Doncaster Parish Church Choir. He left £55,126, and bequests included £300 to the vicar and church wardens of St George's parish church, the annual income to be applied 'for or towards the provision of an annual outing for members of the choir of the said church, where I spent so many happy hours.'

St James' Street showing the old and the new. However, all properties on the left eventually fell victim to demolition.

Looking east at the corner of St James' Terrace and St James's Street with the building currently occupied by the Catholic Club also depicted. C. Smith's grocery premises did not survive the work associated with the construction of the Inner Relief Road.

Two views of St Leger Place, off Dockin Hill Road, which provided a route to and from the local gasworks. All the houses bar the pub, the Stag Inn, have since been demolished. The Stag dates back to at least 1831 when it was titled the Horse & Stag, though the building depicted dates from 1935.

Silver Street with the Essoldo Cinema off centre to the right. On 10 June 1954 the *Doncaster Chronicle* announced that cinemascope, with full stereophonic sound installation was to be introduced during the following week at the Essoldo, Silver Street Doncaster. The film chosen for presentation of this new style of entertainment was *The Flight of the White Heron*, a colour film of a Royal tour which had been described as a picture worth going miles to see. This film was not to be seen anywhere else in the district. Six years later, on 29 December 1960, it was revealed that the Essoldo had re-opened on Boxing Day after being out of action for just over a month because of a fire. Despite the title of the feature film *North to Alaska* there had been no chilly reception from the audiences at the cinema during that Christmas week, and Boxing Day's business was capacity, said manager Ken Scourfield. The cinema had been re-seated in the stalls and the new screen was enlarged. The proscenium and the other area around the stage were re-built. The fire broke out on 20 November and was discovered at around 3 a.m. by George Coward, fitter's mate, of Dockin Hill Road, Doncaster who was going home from work at the time. He saw smoke billowing from the cinema 'and could smell burning wood.' He gave the alarm and Doncaster firemen were quickly on the scene. They had to break a glass panel in the door to enter the cinema. After battling for several hours they managed to get the inferno under control. Mr Coward was to receive a year's pass for two to the cinema as a gesture of thanks and appreciation, said manager Scourfield.

The Essoldo had started its life as a live theatre until 1920 when a changeover was made to motion pictures. In 1932 it was converted into a modern cinema at a cost of around £60,000. Seating capacity was 2,000. In 1947 it became known as the Essoldo.

Station Road looking towards the railway station. C. Wightman JP, the president of the Doncaster Mutual Co-operative and Industrial Society, Ltd, formally opened the Society's new premises in Station Road on Thursday afternoon 27 May 1897. The premises were by far the most costly and important the Society had hitherto built and, it was claimed, ranked amongst the noblest contributions to the architecture of the country for which the movement had been responsible. The building was demolished in the second phase of the Arndale Centre development.

Station Road with the new Co-op and Printing Office Street in the distance. Doncaster Co-operative Society's handsome new store at the St Sepulchre Gate/Printing Office Street junction was opened on Monday 9 December 1940. Sir William Bradshaw, president of the Co-operative Wholesale Society, who opened the premises, spoke of the faith of the pioneers of the Co-operative movement, a faith which he said had been fully justified. The new building was referred to as 'Doncaster's Finest Building', and was an example of the Art Deco style of architecture.

Station Road with Factory Lane in the distance. Mayor Charles Verity and members of Doncaster Corporation formally opened Station Road, amidst pomp and ceremony, on 31 August 1882. The buildings featured in the distance include the Glyn Hotel and the Oriental Chambers.

The news vendor at the Station Road/West Laith Gate junction. Note the 'electronic' Doncaster town guide on the left and the steps leading to the underground lavatories.

Station Road viewed from near the railway station prior to the completion of the second phase of the Arndale Centre and the Inner Relief Road's construction. The Grand Theatre is the only building surviving today from this scene. The business premises featured include those belonging to G.P. Preston & Sons Ltd (tools and fishing tackle), Thirty Five Café (Micklethwaite and Brackburry), M. & G. Confectioners (Mrs D.E. Micklethwaite) and Edwards Motors (Doncaster) Ltd (motor engineers and dealers).

The junction of Princes Street/East Laith Gate and Thorne Road with Christ Church in the distance. Christ Church was designed by Messrs Woodhead and Hurst, in what has been described as the early Gothic Revival style and completed in June 1829. The spire was damaged by lightning in 1836 and again in 1850. Renovation work also took place on the spire during the 1920s.

A view along Union Street which was set out as a new road or highway in 1802. Initially it only extended between St James' Street and Cross Street (merged with Cleveland Street from 1831). By 1840 however it had been extended from its junction with Cleveland Street to St Sepulchre Gate. The business premises of White & Carter, corn and seeds merchants, may be seen on the left. Union Street was cleared by the mid-1960s, yet part of the entrance from St Sepulchre Gate still exists.

Victoria Street with St James' Street and the Shakespeare's Head public house in the distance. Victoria Terrace is to the left. Victoria Street extended between St James' Street and Green Dyke Lane and much of the house building along the thoroughfare took place in stages during the latter half of the nineteenth century. It was cleared by the 1970s.

Two Balby trolleys at the St Sepulchre Gate/Cleveland Street junction. Trolleybuses first operated on the Balby route on 26 July 1931 which became the busiest trolleybus service. Six vehicles usually operated on the route during weekdays with ten on Saturdays. Trolleybus crews often complained that twelve minutes allowed for the outward journey and thirteen for the return was impracticable since the route was very busy and there were sixteen stops to make. Trolleybus operation on the Balby route, service No. 10, was withdrawn on 8 September 1962. The building just behind the trolley on the right was Doncaster's first-purpose built hospital. In later years it became the local YMCA headquarters and was demolished in 1963.

An Edlington Hill Top bus makes a final stop in Young Street before crossing over the busy road into the Waterdale Glasgow Paddocks bus station in readiness for another outward journey. The photograph was taken on 21 December 1963 – the last day buses approached Glasgow Paddocks from this direction.

Two
Show Business

Tommy Roe on stage at the Gaumont. He appeared at the venue on 22 March 1963 along with Chris Montez and the Beatles for one night only. There were two performances one at 6.15pm and another at 8.30pm.

Joe Brown backstage at the Gaumont. (Photograph reproduced by courtesy of Charlie Worsdale)

Helen Shapiro backstage at the Gaumont with local interviewer Carol Roope. Helen Shapiro appeared at the Gaumont. The *Doncaster Gazette* of Thursday 7 February 1963 stated: 'Mr J. Gaukrodger, recently appointed manager of the Gaumont Cinema, Doncaster, put on his first live show there on Tuesday, when top of the bill was teenage international star Helen Shapiro. The young star presented a thirty minute act at each house. Supporting her was a bill which included Kenny Lynch and the dynamic Beatles. Mr Gaukrodger was congratulated on a 'marvellous show by impresario Mr Arthur Howes.' (Photograph reproduced by courtesy of Charlie Worsdale)

The Rolling Stones at the Gaumont. (Photograph reproduced by courtesy of Charlie Worsdale)

John Lennon and George Harrison at the Gaumont, now retitled Odeon. The Beatles made a number of performances in Doncaster during 1963, at St James Street baths and at the Gaumont. These were taken during one of their performances at the Gaumont. (Photograph reproduced by courtesy of Charlie Worsdale)

John Lennon, Paul McCartney and George Harrison pictured at the Gaumont. (Photograph reproduced by courtesy of Charlie Worsdale)

Veteran crooner Bing Crosby at Doncaster races in the 1960s. (Photograph reproduced by courtesy of Charlie Worsdale)

The Bachelors pop group pictured at the First Day of the Spring Meeting at Doncaster Racecourse Tuesday 22 March 1966. (Photograph reproduced by courtesy of Charlie Worsdale)

Cliff Richard at the Gaumont on 30 November 1962. Doncaster deejay Ray Nortrop, wrote in the *New Record Mirror*: 'With coaches for miles around bringing fans into Doncaster, the Cliff Richard tour opened to capacity houses at the Gaumont Cinema – and broke box-office records set up years ago by Bill Haley and the Comets.' He also went on to say that Cliff appeared on stage sporting a bronze tan and in a smart charcoal grey suit. His first number was 'Do You Wanna Dance' which was even excelled by 'The Young Ones', 'The Next Time' and back to fast tempo on 'It'll Be Mine'. (Photograph reproduced by courtesy of Charlie Worsdale)

Freddie Garrity of pop group Freddie and the Dreamers pictured in Baker & Wigfalls record store. (Photograph reproduced by courtesy of Charlie Worsdale)

Doncaster's Ray Nortrop earned a national reputation as a top disc jockey during the 1950s and 1960s. In 1964, at twenty Ray landed what became a marathon residency at the Top Rank suite, Silver Street, which he said 'attracted 2, 000 dancers, weekly.' During December 1965 he won the *Yorkshire Evening Post* Disc Jockey contest which was sponsored by the YEP, Mecca and Pye Records. In time more titles were won and this culminated in him becoming 'Disc Jockey of the Year' in May 1967. It was a contest run nationwide by Radio Luxembourg and EMI Records with the grand final at Croydon being judged by a panel of celebrity judges chaired by Jimmy Young. Ray was frequently sought after by leading impresarios to compere concerts with top stars and introduced the Beatles, Rolling Stones, Kinks, the Animals, Shirley Bassey and Little Richard. Ray appeared on Easy Beat, Thank Your Lucky Stars, Radio Luxembourg, Radio 270 and wrote regularly for the *New Record Mirror*, and had a 14-year association with the *New Musical Express*. He started to promote his own dances in the mid-1960s and operated from offices in the King's Arcade, St Sepulchre Gate.

Local disc-jockey Ray Nortrop pictured at the Top Rank, Silver Street with the She Trinity.

Three
Transport and Doncaster Plant Works

Trolleybus No. 347, seen on a return journey whilst working on the Beckett Road route, passes Albert Drury's shop on Silver Street. On 26 April 1951 the *Doncaster Chronicle* recorded the sudden death of Arnold Drury aged fifty-three. It was said that he sold horse meat in Silver Street and before he held shops of his own, worked for a Baxter Gate butcher. On his twenty-eighth birthday he opened his first shop in French Gate. During the Second World War he served with the NAAFI and for a time managed the Northern Command meat supply depot at Northallerton. 'Drury's FC', a team composed of members of the firm, played in the Doncaster Thursday League for several seasons. Arnold Drury was well known by taxi drivers and always arrived and left work in a taxi.

Trolleybus No. 380 has just passed the Christ Church Road/Netherhall Road junction whilst on the return journey from Beckett Road. The last trolleybus to operate in Doncaster worked on the Beckett Road route on 14 December 1963.

A fine group of motorbuses and trolleybuses providing the public with transport to and from Arksey, Bentley and Skellow from the town centre terminus on North Bridge. The first operational trolley service ran on the Bentley route on 22 August 1928 from this bus stand built on North Bridge. Doncaster Corporation purchased four vehicles from Garretts of Leiston and four from Karriers of Luton (all three axle vehicles) to begin the service. On the whole it was claimed that trolleys were very popular with the Doncaster public as they provided a smooth and comfortable ride in comparison with the trams and early motorbuses.

Two trolleys pass near the Bridge Hotel. Note that the Toby Jug public house is under construction on the left. The pub opened on 2 November 1955 and replaced the 'George & Dragon' situated on the opposite side of the road. The pub has since been demolished.

A motorbus on its return journey from Selby via Askern passes along Marsh Gate on its way to the town centre terminus on 14 August 1967.

The Marsh Gate terminus seen here on 19 August 1967.

A Doncaster Corporation clippie, pausing for a cigarette break.

Trolleybus No. 362 glides along Carr House Road whilst on the Hyde Park route. When Carr House Road was transformed during the 1930s into a main road it enabled both the Racecourse and Hyde Park trolley routes to become circular routes. For much of the time the Hyde Park trolleys began their services in front of the Co-operative Society Emporium at the St Sepulchre Gate/Printing Office Street junction. Each 'circular' journey on the Hyde Park route took twenty minutes and normally two buses operated on the service.

The Doncaster Corporation overhead tower wagon is pictured at the Catherine Street/Gill Street junction as trolleybus No. 373 passes by on 9 January 1955. This thoroughfare was once part of the Hyde Park/Racecourse trolleybus routes. Catherine Street was laid out in the mid-1860s as a link between Waterdale and Hyde Park. The name is derived from Catherine Mottram (née Gill), a former owner of the land through which it once cut. Whilst the houses on Catherine Street have been demolished, the route has been widened and renamed Trafford Way and is still part of a public transport system.

Trolleybus No. 358 seen in traffic on St Sepulchre Gate West on 31 December 1955.

Trolleybus No. 367 passes the Odeon cinema in Hall Gate on 25 September 1955 whilst working on the Racecourse route. Other features include Elvin's Cafe and Grace's (Hosiery).

A Stainforth and Dunscroft bus at the Thorne Road/East Laith Gate junction.

The Waterdale bus station looking towards the Coal House (now Council House). This are has since become a car park.

A group of Yorkshire Traction buses pictured outside the old West Riding Police building in Station Road on 3 November 1954.

Bill Woollner (right) a chargeman in the Plant Works' B1 Shop is seen training an apprentice fitter/turner on 2 February 1959.

An apprentice is pictured carrying out tracing work in the Plant Works' drawing office on 29 September 1956.

The Plant Works' Carriage & Wagon Carnival Parade, pictured here, always began from this point near the railway station and terminated at Eden Grove sports ground, Hexthorpe. This view was taken on 29 May 1954.

The Plant Works' Centenary celebrations were held over the weekend 19-20 September 1953.

The Plant Works' Centenary celebrations; the opening ceremony was performed by R.A. Riddles.

The Plant Works' Centenary celebrations.

The prototype Deltic locomotive in Doncaster station. The initial trials of the locomotive began in the mid-1950s and it then worked for a while between Liverpool and London. A little later, in January 1959, it was transferred to the Eastern Region where it worked the East Coast Services. After suffering a traction motor failure in 1961 it was not refurbished until two years later and then transferred by a road vehicle to the Science Museum in South Kensington on 28 April 1963.

Class A4 locomotive No. 60006 Sir Ralph Wedgwood at Doncaster Station during the early 1960s.

Plant Works Inspectors Michael Crabtree (extreme left) and Hugh Parkin (extreme right), photographed with students from Darlington undertaking a short Works course on 5 April 1967.

Interior view of the Plant Works Stores accounting department during the 1960s.

The frontage to Doncaster railway station which was built in the late 1930s.

View in the Waterdale bus station featuring a Leon Motorbus Co. vehicle. In the distance Beechfield House may seen.

Trolleybus No. 382 is seen at Clock Corner on Saturday 15 May 1955 whilst working on the Bentley route. Boots' premises may be seen in the background before being transformed into the new Arndale Centre.

Four

Commercial

An advertisement of E. & G. Charlesworth's featuring the Zephyr Six.

CLAYBOURN'S *"The Car People"*

Your natural choice

for everything in the

Service of Motoring

Hall Gate = Doncaster

PHONE DONCASTER 3414

The Claybourn business began at Askern around 1918, when a bicycle and motor cycle repair shop was opened by Jack Ernest Claybourn. About four years later, he established a motor-garage on Askern's Doncaster Road. The business went from strength to strength, and in 1931 he gradually took over buildings in Hall Gate, Doncaster, when the car showrooms originally held four vehicles. He eventually acquired the whole property and in the early days had the agency for Armstrong Siddely, Morrison Electric, Jowitt and Lanchester. During the First World War, E. Claybourn was a sergeant mechanic in the Royal Flying Corps and his association with the Air force was renewed in the Second World War when the company was engaged in making aircraft parts for the Fairey Swordfish at their Hall Gate premises. From the 1960s they dealt in Singer, Hillman Humber, Sunbeam, Austin, Morris, Daimler and Riley. A service department was established in 1963 but seven years later moved to new larger premises near the Balby Bridge roundabout. At the same time the Hall Gate property was closed and the sales side of the business was concentrated in Princes Street. This continued until 1978 when the new car showrooms were erected at Balby Bridge. When this occurred the Princes Street premises were vacated and the entire Claybourn operation was concentrated at Balby. In 1987, Graham Claybourn, the founder's son, sold the business.

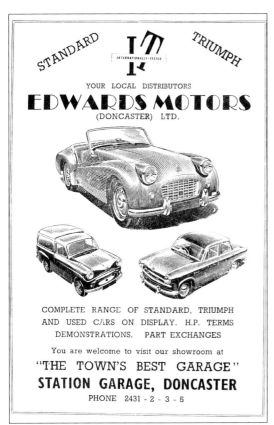

Above left: An advertisement for Edwards' Motors of Station Road, Doncaster.

Above right: In 1959, it was disclosed that Lines Bros of London were buying the business of Mellers (Dolls Hospital) Hall Gate for an undisclosed figure. Mr and Mrs Grenville Meller, the proprietors, were retiring from business. The first Meller shop dealing with toys was opened in Doncaster around 1863. The business also dealt with undertaking and cabinet making and was run by Charles Meller and his son Charles Edward (known as Ted). The business premises were in the Market Place, near the Scot Lane corner, until around 1926; they were then demolished due to the Scot Lane widening scheme. A new shop was subsequently occupied in Hall Gate. When I interviewed Leila Meller, Grenville's wife, some years ago, she told me: 'I think that father-in-law [Ted] started a toy shop, or more specifically the Dolls Hospital as a result of him buying a huge consignment of damaged dolls. By swapping various limbs and things around he was able to make complete dolls. He obviously thought the idea of a Dolls Hospital was novel and unique and nobody else in the town at that time was doing that sort of thing. There was quite a bit of money in it too since many of the more expensive dolls which needed repairing were owned by children of the wealthy.' Lines Bros of Merton, south–west London, who had shops and interests in a number of areas, continued the business for a time. The premises are currently occupied by solicitors Bridge Sanderson & Co.

In December 1951, a Doncaster garage which had been the local depot for J. Bullock and Sons (1928) Ltd since 1933, and had continued in use as a depot since the firm's amalgamation with the West Riding Automobile Co. Ltd, over a year earlier was to be sold by public auction. A spokesman of the West Riding Automobile Co. said that the Doncaster depot was being cut out to effect economies in operational costs and that the former staff of 40 workers had found or had been found other jobs.

According to an article in 1962, Carver's shoe shop, in the Market Place, Doncaster, 'was very big', extending back nearly 160 feet from the pavement, and containing 12 rooms (bursting with thousands of shoes). Harold Carver, who represented the second generation of his family to run the business was born in the shop. When he was a child the market was his playground. The first man to sell shoes there was Cllr. E. Edgar, who was responsible for introducing the first water mains in Doncaster. He took the shop in 1873. Before that it had been a grocery and a hardware store. In 1894 the first Carver-Joseph came into the business. Trained as a shoemaker at Wakefield, he married his boss's daughter and when he had built up sufficient capital came to Doncaster and bought Cllr Edgar's business.

Market Place showing the Dogs' Hotel, Dix's restaurant and the Market Tavern. George Brooks, born in 1907, was a native of Doncaster and for more than twenty years worked as a blacksmith at the town's railway Plant Works, retiring through ill health in 1946. Earlier, in 1937, he and his wife became joint proprietors of Dix's Cafe, Market Place, Doncaster. He died in 1952 and The Market Tavern closed around 1978.

Clark of Retford (cleaners) at No. 49 Market Place and J.W. Brooke & Sons (leather factors) at No. 50.

Both pictures show shops on the northern side of the Market Place. In the post-war years there were plans to redevelop the market and demolish some of its fine structures, but fortunately these were never carried out. The Black Bull public house on the extreme left in the top picture was once tenanted by the late Alick Jeffrey, arguably the town's most famous footballer.

In 1941, after serving with the forces during the Second World War, Albert Warner was invalided out and faced with the question, 'Where do I go from here?'. He was said to have limited resources but had a great deal of encouragement and practical help from his wife Gladys to open a wet fish and fruit shop in Yarborough Terrace. Shortly afterwards they secured their first market stall on Doncaster market, seen here during the 1960s. Their sons, Brian and Bernard followed their parents into the business. The business expanded with further market stalls in Doncaster, Rotherham and Ashby, and in 1972 the opening of a wholesale warehouse on Grey Friars Road (later York Road).

Row of commercial premises on High Street. They include Jas Woodhouse & Sons (furnishers) in the Westminster Arcade, Rayner (opticians) and Vickers & Son.

L. Spero's antiques and fine arts premises.

Cockney Frank Sverdloff, born in 1893, was taken to the Ukraine at the age of six by his mother following the death of his father. He married in Russia and lived through the Revolution. He came back to England with his wife Rosa and daughter Gladys in 1919. Frank, who was then twenty-six, found it difficult leaving Russia. His British birth certificate and passport were confiscated, but he got replacements from the British Consul and was able to leave. He and his family came to live in Doncaster, where he was a pedlar for some time, before opening a stall in the market. Despite early difficulties with the language, Frank managed to do well in business. He opened a small shop in the front parlour of his home in Catherine Street and then expanded his business to found the Solo chain. Frank and his family moved home to Bessacarr and then to Moorland Court, Lawn Road. Frank remained managing director of Solo in Market Place, Doncaster, until his death in a Sheffield nursing home in 1975, aged eighty-two. His wife had died four years earlier.

F. Stone, Lighting and Radio Ltd, whose business premises were on Baxter Gate.

During November 1978, it was announced that Sawyers – the well-known DIY 'Mecca', at the Trafford Way/St Sepulchre Gate West junction – was to close in the New Year. All the store's twenty-three workers were to lose their jobs because of what the company described as a deteriorating trading position. One piece of good news was that Gent's, the lingerie manufacturer, who already operated on other floors of the building occupied by the DIY company, were to take over the latter's premises. Sawyers' store manager, Roy Travis explained: 'The plain fact of the matter is our trading position has not been very good lately.' He emphasized that competition had played its part, but also blamed the long-standing effect on trade of the nearby Inner Relief Road (Trafford Way). 'There is no doubt about it, the road effected our custom,' he said. 'It cut us off from the town centre and put people off from making the effort to come to us'. Sawyers began trading in Doncaster in 1946.

High Street featuring Rhodes & Rosslyn (outfitters) and Blindells Ltd (footwear).

Scarborough Bros' premises in St Sepulchre Gate pictured shortly before demolition in the early 1960s for the Inner Relief Road. Curtis Scarborough was a native of Billingley, Lincs, and at the age of sixteen started work with his uncle, James Scarborough, who was the founder of the firm of wholesale fruit and potato merchants, St Sepulchre Gate. When his uncle died Curtis Scarborough took over the business and took into partnership with him George Stacey, one of the employees, the business being carried on under the name of Scarborough & Stacey. Scarborough retired from active participation in the business in 1890, but for some years had some dealings with potato growers in Yorkshire and Lincolnshire. The business was taken over by Preston Scarborough, and later by the latter's sons. Curtis Scarborough died aged eighty-three on Thursday 9 July 1925, at his residence, No. 42 Spring Gardens, Doncaster. The *Doncaster Review* of March 1897 noted that Mr Preston Scarborough had opened 'his new premises in St Sepulchre Gate and has introduced the electric light for illuminating purposes, being in fact the first private tradesman to do so in Doncaster...'

On Monday, 4 December 1950 it was reported that the funeral took place, at the Jewish cemetery at Rose Hill, of Samuel Morris, twice mayor of the town, prominent businessman and racehorse owner. He was for many years senior partner of S. & H. Morris Ltd, Doncaster, wallpaper manufacturers and retailers, and a director of Wallpaper Manufacturers Ltd of London and Manchester. At the age of thirteen, Morris made his first move which was to bring him success. He left home in Sheffield to assist in the loading of ponies for his uncle at Hull, but instead of returning home as he should have done, he went to New York in the boat carrying the ponies. He remained in New York for two years, earning 10 dollars a week for exercising race horses and doing general duties as a stable lad before returning to his family in Sheffield. It was shortly afterwards that he made his first appearance in Doncaster – selling wallpaper from a stall in the Market Place. The partner with him in that enterprise was his brother Hyman Morris who became Lord Mayor of Leeds in 1941-42. Samuel Morris eventually opened a shop at the West Street/St Sepulchre Gate corner in 1890. The firm expanded and at one time had five shops in Doncaster alone, with another twenty shops in other parts of the country including Blackpool, Boston, Chester, Chesterfield, and Crewe. The business survived in Doncaster until recent times.

Two views of Priestnall's cafés. Joseph William Priestnall was born at Clay Cross, near Chesterfield, but later lived in Doncaster for forty years. For thirty-five years he was in the catering business, and owned three cafés in the town in addition to being an ice-cream manufacturer. It was said that J. Priestnall did a large amount of charity work anonymously, sometimes even without telling his family. Every year he provided a treat for old folk, a trip to the seaside, or a theatre visit, followed by a supper at his café. At Christmas 1952, in addition to giving toys, sweets and ice cream to children in Doncaster infirmary and council homes, he gave food for a party of crippled children from Hesley Hall, given by US airmen at Lindholme. He died aged fifty-nine in May 1953.

The frontage of Peerage Antiques
in Bennetthorpe.

L. Parker and his newsagent's and tobacconist's shop at No. 74 Cemetery Road. Many houses
on Cemetery Road were demolished between 1971 and 1973. A group however were retained
at the southern end of the street because they allegedly had been built to a higher standard than
the others. These now form Milton walk.

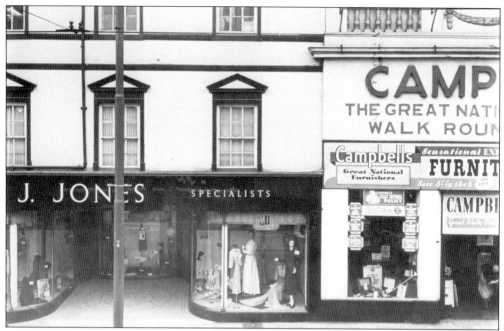

J. Jones (1920) Ltd (gowns and costumes) at No. 42 High Street and Campbells, the house furnishers, at No. 43 are featured in this view.

Ken Soper, born in 1920, set up a glass business on leaving the Navy after the Second World War. His first premises were on Doncaster market, then he moved to Cleveland Street, selling glass and mirrors which they manufactured on the premises. His son Mick entered the business after leaving Hyde Park school at the age of fifteen. The business relocated to Arksey Lane in 1964 when the Cleveland Street shop was cleared for redevelopment in the area. Ken Soper died in 1970 and Mick carried on the business along with the apprentices trained by his father. In 1980, Sopers, as the firm is popularly known, diversified into DIY, establishing another shop on Bentley Road. Two years later, Mick's wife, Angie, opened a jewellery shop in premises adjacent to the Arksey Lane business and this has proved to be very successful, attracting customers from a wide radius.

Goodlys store in French Gate.
Note that Davy's café is adjacent
on the left.

Months of planning came to fruition as crowds flocked in, and good luck telegrams arrived, at the
new Boots branch which opened in the Arndale (now French Gate) Centre on Friday 25 July 1968.
The branch, which had moved across the road from Clock Corner, was the second largest chain
store to move into the Arndale Centre, joining British Home Stores which had opened almost two
years earlier. The picture shows part of the old Boots which fronted on to Baxter Gate.

Timothy Whites (chemists) store in the Market Place.

The sale of Messrs Postlethwaite & Stacey's shop in Hall Gate, Doncaster, during 1961 meant the end of a furnishing business which had been in the same two families for around sixty years. The firm operated from a site near the entrance to Bradford Row. It was founded in 1897 by carpet salesman John Postlethwaite and Charles Lumley with premises in Retford. Two years later they opened a showroom in Doncaster's Oriental Chambers in Station Road, and in 1900 they rented No. 16 Hall Gate, using the front room as a show room and shop. In the same year Arthur Stacey, previously assistant surveyor to Doncaster Corporation, joined the firm and in 1904, when the original partnership was dissolved, it became Postlethwaite & Stacey. The business was considerably expanded in 1911 when the adjoining property was acquired.

In November 1949 it was reported that ice-cream and dairy equipment, invented and manufactured by a young Doncaster ex-serviceman, Frederick James Arrand, was to be exported to Holland and the West Indies. Also, substantial home orders which he secured in four days at the Dairy Show at Olympia, were making a success story for him. Leaving the Army, in which he had served in France, the Middle East, Sicily, and Italy, as medically unfit in 1944, F.J. Arrand, then 24, took a job as a welder at a Doncaster factory. In his spare time he was busy inventing an ice-cream conservator, and a few months after the end of the war he went into business on his own account. He made the conservator on a small scale, with only a boy and one part-time assistant in a small Spring Gardens workshop (the frontage is seen here). It was a success and later from a factory in Nelson Street, Hyde Park, F.J. Arrand and his staff of 22 turned out refrigeration and ventilation equipment and accepted welding contracts. At another workshop in Spring Gardens F.J. Arrand ran a joinery business, and was managing director of a business which turned out cold room cabinets.

A member of the Moate family (builders and contractors) pictured with one of the business vehicles in the 1960s. Information on the van indicates that the firm was established in 1880 and located in Cunningham Road.

David and Michael Cuttriss ran a model shop first in Cleveland Street (seen here) and later in Duke Street. Their success was 'inextricably linked with an upsurge in interest in modelling, and a growth in the number of manufacturers producing aeroplane kits, train sets and toys.' Their business started around 1936 with Michael selling balsa wood, tissue and glue for people to make model aeroplanes. David helped him and their early customers were largely Doncaster Model Flying Club members. The war subsequently intervened, though when both brothers returned from service life, they took control of their business again, taking over space in their father's Cleveland Street garage. They embarked into the world of model railways around 1949 becoming agents for Trix twin trains. The great craze for plastic kits started in the early 1950s with the introduction of Airfix's classic range of products. In 1964 the brothers moved to Duke Street following redevelopment in the Cleveland Street area. By 1983, Michael was sixty-one and 'ready for retirement.' David, who was ill that year, became convinced that it might be a good idea for him too. Consequently, Cuttriss' closed in November 1983.

The business of motorcycle dealers W. Cusworth (Doncaster) Ltd was founded by the late W.E. Clark before the turn of the last century. It was acquired by W. Cusworth (Doncaster) Ltd shortly after the Second World War. For some time the Company had its main showroom in Hall Gate, Doncaster, and a warehouse behind cottages in Whitaker Street/Princegate. In 1958/9 the latter were demolished to make way for new buildings. The manager at this time was W. Cusworth, the architect of the new building Dennis E. Wilburn, and the main contractors J.H. Gilbert Ltd. The new buildings were in fact, the first to be erected in the new shopping area becoming known as the Waterdale Centre. Over Easter week 1959, Cusworth's staged a special motorcycle exhibition to celebrate the opening of the new premises. On W. Cusworth's retirement during the late 1960s, Henry Hall and three other employees bought the business. Later, Henry bought out the three other partners at different times over the following 15 years, so that by the early 1980s, he was the sole owner. In 1991, Henry retired himself from the business, allowing son Chris to take control.

A Fairway store at the Silver Street/Bowers Fold Corner photographed during the 1960s. Fairway Food Markets was founded by Harry Round, a noted character in his day. On 30 May 1983 it was announced that Fairway, Doncaster's oldest-established supermarket chain, was to be sold for around £1 million. The family firm of eight Doncaster food stores was being bought by the Milton Keynes-based company, Linfood Holdings. According to Fairway's joint managing director Michael Round, the firm employed around 400 and he understood that Linfood was not intending to make any large-scale redundancies. However, it was mentioned that the presentation and merchandising of the stores may be slightly changed to bring them in line with other outlets owned by Linfood. At the time of the takeover the family firm was run by Michael and his two brothers. Fairway's eight shops included several town centre sites.

View of Baxter Gate looking towards the Market Place.

On Thursday 21 June 1961, it was announced that Davy's shop and restaurant in French Gate would close at the weekend and would be pulled down. The property had been acquired by the Arndale Trust. The announcement of the impending closure of Davy's was made by the managing director J. Willows who had called the staff together and told them they would be paid compensation according to the number of years service they had with the company. Printed notices were placed on the café tables saying that owing to the redevelopment scheme of the area the company's shop in Scot Lane would continue to operate as usual. The French Gate shop, which was established in 1924, covered about a thousand square feet, with the restaurant seating around 108 above and a bakery at the rear. Some of the employees were in tears when they were told of the closure.

Cleveland Street near the junction with Printing Office Street to the left. This row of properties was formerly known as King Charles Terrace.

Shops on Cleveland Street near the junction with Portland Place.

In November 1961, the father and son owners of Bon Marché (Doncaster) Ltd, Archie and David Cramer, boasted that they had served over a quarter of a million satisfied customers since establishing the firm nine years earlier. Plus their Market Place store had just been extended and altered to give more than double the amount of selling space. They added that their customers did not only come from Doncaster and the surrounding area but from Leeds, Sheffield, Rotherham and especially from Scunthorpe. 'We even had a lady who came from Scotland because she had bought a coat a few years ago when she had been passing through the town and it was such good value she wanted another one from us,' said David Cramer, the twenty-six year old director of the firm, who left university to take over the running of the business because of the ill-health of his father, Archie Cramer, who founded it. D. Cramer visited manufacturers in London, Nottingham, Manchester and Leicester, to buy direct from them, so that he could offer remarkable values, together with up-to-date styles.

Funeral directors Steadman & Sons' business premises on Cleveland Street. In 1962 Steadmans transferred their business premises to Balby Road having outgrown the town centre property.

During October 1988 it was announced that one of the town's oldest-established firms, booksellers and stationers Taylor & Colbridge in Hall Gate was to close. Taylor & Colbridge opened around 1920 in St Sepulchre Gate (seen here about 1966), and the closure meant that around eight people would lose their jobs. Manager Gordon Pratt blamed the closure on dwindling trade. 'Two years ago we moved from St Sepulchre Gate where we had been for more than sixty years. Unfortunately the move has not worked out,' he said. The shop was owned by a Leeds firm, commercial stationers Jowett & Sowry, who bought out Mr Colbridge in the 1930s. The Hall Gate shop closed on 26 November 1988.

Vehicles pictured at the rear of Ford Motor Co. dealers, E & G. Charlesworth's premises in Bennetthorpe.

The glass and china business of A. Porter & Sons was established in Barnsley in 1872. Around 1887, William Porter moved to Doncaster and first opened premises in French Gate, and later in the Market Place.

Five
Events

A gathering round the war memorial in Bennetthorpe during November 1958. *The Doncaster Chronicle* of Thursday 13 November 1958 reported: 'At Doncaster there was a wreath laying ceremony at the War Memorial, Bennetthorpe. Afterwards the mayor (Cllr. A. Harvey) and Wing Commander Grant of R.A.F. Finningley, took the salute at the Mansion House. The vicar of Doncaster (Canon H.G.G. Herklots) conducted a service in the Parish Church'.

Laurence Michael Harvey (6th Earl of Rosse) lays the foundation stone for the new Museum and Art Gallery in Chequer Road on 10 April 1962.

The upstairs galleries at the museum and art gallery shortly after opening.

A band concert in the front gardens of the old Museum and Art Gallery which was once housed in Beechfield House, Waterdale.

It's all hands to the pumps as a fire takes hold of Gadsby's Timber and Hardware store at the Cleveland Street/Spring Gardens corner.

A Sikh wedding in Upper Oxford Street, now demolished.

Six
Pubs and Hotels

The new Turf Tavern opened in the Golden Acres project at Waterdale, at the Spring Gardens/St James Street junction on Tuesday 12 December 1967. It carried on the history and name of the famous early nineteenth century Turf Tavern at the corner of Bentinck Street/St James' Street (seen here). The Turf Tavern of the 1960s was described as a luxurious new drinking and dining venue for Doncaster, the latest from the John Smith's brewery stable, combining the grace and comfort of a sedate age with the style and convenience of modern times. The old Turf figured prominently in horse-racing in the early nineteenth century. Stables there housed several winners of the Doncaster St Leger and other classics of the turf and for several years the stud of Lord George Bentinck was stabled there.

The Shakespeare's Head at the St Sepulchre Gate/St James' Street junction closed on 16 August 1965.

Last pints were pulled at the old Wellington Inn at a corner of Doncaster Market Place on Monday 30 March 1964. The Wellington had met its Waterloo – beaten by progress. Soon it would be a heap of rubble before making way for a shopping development. It was a sad time on that Monday night when the landlord John Hughes and his wife Hilda called, 'Time gentlemen please' for the last time. However the break did have a compensation; the couple were able to have a holiday together for the first time in twenty-eight years. Luckily the Wellington was not to be lost to the site altogether, a new 'underground' pub, was to be included in the new development, and it was planned that John and his wife were to be in charge. The Wellington had played its part in the town's history, but although it had an old world appearance during its last fifty years, it had been considerably altered around 1913, and it was not originally called the Wellington. Its former name was the Mitre, and dated back to at least 1719. It probably changed its title with the spate of 'Wellingtons' up and down the country to commemorate the victories and achievements of the famous soldier, particularly after the defeat of Napoleon in 1815. The Underground opened on 21 December 1964, and was re-named Wellington Vaults on 8 March 1983.

For a period the Reindeer Vaults were the property of the Planet Trading Company, who also owned the Danum Hotel on the opposite side of the road.

In May 1960 the St Sepulchre Gate property, formerly the Good Woman Hotel, was the latest section of old Doncaster to pass into the hands of a modern development company. The property, together with two shops facing St Sepulchre Gate and one facing West Laith Gate, was sold at an auction conducted by Peter Welborne, a partner in the Doncaster firm of D.L. Staniland & Co., estate agents. It was sold for £30,000 to H.E. Gregory, a Leeds estate agent in Leeds, acting on behalf of Land Improvements Ltd of Bournemouth. The Good Woman Hotel, which lost its licence in 1938, had been used as a café, small shop and transport hotel.

Interior views of the Elephant Hotel on St Sepulchre Gate. The hotel closed on Saturday 26 January 1974. At the time of its closure the Elephant boasted the last men only bar in Doncaster. Its windows still displayed the stained glass installed when the hotel was built in 1914.

On Thursday 10 December 1962, brewers Richard Whitaker & Sons Ltd opened their redeveloped public house 'Beethams' (formerly George & Dragon) at the St George Gate/Baxter Gate corner. Among the guests at the official opening ceremony was Bill Acaster, former licensee of the old George & Dragon which was demolished to make way for the new public house, forming part of a shop and office development. Company chairman Herbert Whittaker, described the building of the new pub as unique, thanking all those connected with the scheme, including Doncaster Corporation. He said the name of 'Beethams' had been chosen because the old George & Dragon was more familiarly known by that name than the proper title. Mrs Beetham, former owner of the site, was unable to be present. The public facilities of the new licensed premises were a public bar at ground level and a 'dive' lounge bar. Lunch–time catering and evening snacks were to be a feature of the new pub. Ex-RAF member John McGuiness, was appointed 'mine host.' In subsequent years the premises have become known as the Gatehouse/Mayfair Cafe Bars & Cellars. The picture here shows the old building.

'Time Gents Please,' was called for the last time on Saturday 29 December 1962 at the Angel & Royal Hotel, French Gate. For the ancient 28 bedroom hotel, which had ceased to be a residential hotel several years earlier, was due to be demolished for the Arndale (now French Gate) Centre. Previously, the Angel was on the opposite site of the street, where the Guildhall stood. Many famous people had stayed at the Angel, including Queen Victoria and Charles Dickens. The last pints were pulled at 11.30-the New Year's Eve extension had been brought forward-and regulars 'dug in' to a huge iced cake baked by a customer to commemorate the closing. The manager, John Macdonald, was moving to the Fitzwilliam Arms.

'View from the North Bridge with the Volunteer public house in the foreground and St George's church in the distance. The pub, which could be traced back with the title of the Volunteer to at least 1805, closed in 1961 and the licence was transferred to the Benbow on Armthorpe Road. It had existed as the Skinners Arms from at least 1760.

Doncaster's first television licence for a public house was granted to the Alma Inn, St Sepulchre Gate, at Doncaster Borough Court on Monday 5 March 1951. Superintendent W.T. Davies argued that if television in public houses meant subdued lighting and crowding round the sets, the Bench ought to consider refusing applications. Licensee Mr R. Smith responded that he believed his television set, which was to be installed in the Alma's smoke room, would not need subdued lights. Describing the application as a 'new departure', the chairman (Mr J. Barber) said the Bench granted the application with some hesitancy, perhaps because of the novelty! Photograph reproduced by courtesy of Stan Parker who was the last licensee at the pub when it closed in 1966.

Alma Athletic F.C. pictured during the 1958-59 season.

A link with Doncaster's past was broken on Monday 2 August 1965 when the Thatched House Hotel at the Camden Street/St Sepulchre Gate corner closed for the last time before its demolition to make way for road improvements. Many customers, who had regularly sunk pints at the pub thronged the three rooms to bid farewell to the licensee Dennis Hayhurst and his wife Joan, who two days later took over the Station Hotel, Treeton.

William Connell, a regular for twenty-five years said he was sorry the hotel was closing: 'It has always been a friendly house – just like a family – and several generations have been represented among the customers.' Dennis Hayhurst, the pub's tenant for over four years said he regretted leaving as he had made many friends. He thought the public house should not have to be demolished; it could have been taken further back from the proposed road widening. A remarkable feature of the trade was that people who had moved to outlying districts since their houses had been demolished had maintained their custom, many travelling a fair distance to do so. Dave Mitchell, captain of the darts team, presented a clock to Mr and Mrs Hayhurst on behalf of the darts club and regular customers.

Seven
Aerial Views

Aerial view taken in June 1951 looking over the North Bridge, Doncaster Railway Station and Plant Railway Works towards Cusworth. Some of the main buildings of the Plant Works are discernible here including the Carriage Works, Crimpsall Workshops, New Erecting Shop and North Carriage Shed. Note that the Marsh Gate Power Station is under construction on the right.

A bird's eye view from the St George's church tower. Ye Olde Crown Hotel, dating from at least 1795 and rebuilt around 1902, is in the foreground. Joseph Rank's (formerly Hanley's) flour mill and Low Fisher Gate occupy the middle distance.

Duke Street looking towards Cleveland Street and Baker Street. Cuttriss's model shop may be seen in the distance on Cleveland Street. Before being laid out with houses, Duke Street was known as Ropers Walk. A large number of the Duke Street houses were cleared in the mid-1930s. This picture shows the area before redevelopment during the 1960s.

Aerial view from above Leicester Avenue with the racecourse in the distance. At the end of Leicester Avenue the Corporation bus depot and fire station may be seen. Doncaster Corporation's Watch Committee first considered the closing of the Factory Lane fire station in 1931, but it was not until the new fire station in Lonsdale Avenue (seen here) was opened on 10 March 1937 that this took place. The Home Office in this year stopped the use of police officers as firemen and the new station included five flats for five full-time firemen. The chief constable gave up his responsibilities and a fire superintendent was appointed full time.

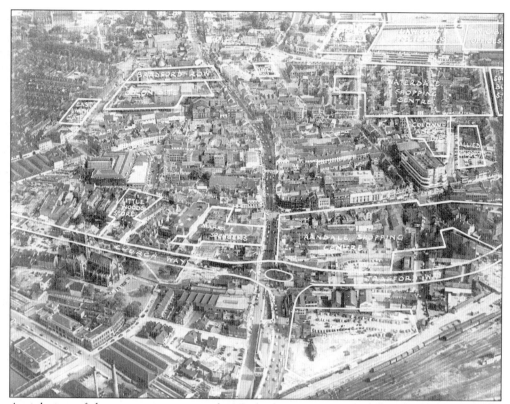

Aerial view of the town centre around 1958 looking southwards from North Bridge along French Gate, High Street and Hall Gate. Some of the main developments which took place in the ensuing years are noted.

Glasgow Paddocks is in the foreground and York Road leads into the distance.

An aerial view of Doncaster Plant Works with the Marsh Gate Power Station dominating the centre of the picture.

Eight

Redevelopment

St James' Street with St James' Terrace in the distance on the left.

Demolition of the old Turf Tavern.

The old and new Staff of Life public houses are pictured alongside each other in the mid 1960s. The old premises at the Whittaker Street/Young Street corner had been in existence from at least 1862.

Two views of redevelopments along Cleveland Street. The bottom photograph shows the Spring Gardens Methodist chapel being demolished.

A view of living conditions in yards off St Sepulchre Gate before, some would say, long–awaited demolition.

Sweeping away the old and building the new. After house and commercial clearance on Cleveland Street, new flats are under construction during the early 1960s. The Corporation Taps public house may be seen in the distance.

Oxford Place at the junction with St James' Street shortly before demolition. Most of the thirty-two Oxford Place terraced houses were erected between 1869 and 1872. The even numbers (2-34) were on the western side, odds (1-29) on the east. The demolition of Oxford Place curiously stretched over two compulsory purchase orders. The western side was incorporated in the Central area Number 5 CPO 1966, the eastern side and the large Methodist chapel in the Central area Number 6 CPO 1968.

The top picture shows one of the entrances to the Sandhouse tunnels off Victoria Street. The illustration below shows one of the tunnels and some of the carvings within them. The Sandhouse was formerly one of Doncaster's Victorian marvels. Reports of the Doncaster Corporation's intention to clear the remains of the Sandhouse site in the 1960s prompted Richard Storry, a Fellow of St Anthony's College, Oxford, to write one of several letters to the *Doncaster Press* recalling the Sandhouse and deploring its demise. In his view: 'To have turned that green hollow into a refuse dump was an act of barbaric stupidity. To build high-rise flats over the warren of the Catacombs would seem... to be less barbaric but, perhaps, hardly less stupid.'

Work is taking place on the construction of Chappell Drive, a new wholesale market area off Church Way. Note the gasworks on the left.

The new roundabout takes shape at the junction of North Bridge Road/Trafford Street (renamed Trafford Way) and Church Way. At a meeting of the Doncaster Corporation's Highways and Public Works Committee on 2 June 1966, it was recommended that 'the section of the inner relief road from North Bridge to Cleveland Street be renamed 'Trafford Way.' Originally there was an intention to erect a flyover at the French Gate end of Trafford Street and one at the junction with Cleveland street, to segregate through traffic from internal traffic. However this was never carried out.

View along Church View from Church Way, with Edwards Motor Co.'s new premises under construction on the left.

Church Way with the old trades club in the distance on North Bridge Road. The old club had to be demolished to make way for the new inner ring road. The official opening of the new trades club took place on 24 September 1969 and was performed by the Rt Hon. Ray Gunter MP. In the souvenir booklet produced for the opening ceremony it was stated: 'An early concept was to establish a strong relationship between the new club building, bus station and multi-storey car park to be erected on the adjoining site and an additional requirement was introduced to provide public facilities administered by the Corporation at the lower ground floor level related to the bus station.'

Two more views from the early 1960s looking from St James' Street over to Cleveland Street. Much of the vacant area was subsequently occupied with high-rise flats.

St James' Street looking towards St Sepulchre Gate with the St John Street Co-op on the right
One of the vans on the left belongs to J & J. H Peters.

The new Southern bus station under construction.

The Corporation Brewery formerly owned by the Ream family.

Demolition on Spring Gardens near the Cleveland Street junction. The Scarborough Arms on the corner closed in June 1962. The licence was subsequently transferred to the Paddock, at Cantley.

Part of the Golden Acres development under construction during the 1960s. It is now more familiarly known as the Waterdale Shopping Centre. Initially, the Golden Acres was intended to cover the area bounded by Spring Gardens, Waterdale Wood Street and Cleveland Street. Demolition not only occurred along the area's periphery, but also within it, affecting Young Street, Baker Street, Pavilion street and Whitaker Street. Consequently many families sought alternative housing and traders new locations. There was also a plan to erect two six-story blocks of flats, but this was abandoned in favour of building maisonettes, ie. dwelling units/flats above some of the shops.

On 18 January 1962, it was reported that demolition work had begun to make way for a £250,000 redevelopment of the old Reindeer Hotel site at the Cleveland Street/Hall Gate junction. It was proposed that the scheme would provide a big department store and showrooms and was expected to be completed in about a year. Demolition of the old property, formerly occupied by Raymond's Gowns, the gentleman's outfitters of Harold Kelsey Ltd, and the hotel was expected to take about six weeks and a part of the proposed three-storey new building had already been let to a multiple firm of costumiers.

One of the great events of the Co-operative movement in Doncaster was the opening of the new shops, lecture hall, offices, library, and reading room which the society built in 1893 at the John Street/Cleveland Street junction. The building was designed by Herbert Athron and the work was executed by Messrs H. Arnold & Son, taking about 12 months to complete. The style of the building was described as Free Classic, the main elevations being faced with pressed bricks, with terracotta piers to the shop windows and principal entrance doors. In the basement of the building were cellars for the storage of meat, a furniture show room, glass and china show room, boot and shoe repairing shop and heating chamber. On the ground floor there were four large shops; and on the first floor the reading room, library, offices, and committee room were located. On the second floor was an assembly room capable of holding 600 people. The building is seen here being demolished during the 1960s.

Redevelopment along Cleveland Street with the YMCA on the right and the Thatched House pub on the left.

View of the Old Exchange Brewery in Hudson Mews off Cleveland Street. The brewery was rebuilt in 1897 and attached to the Old Exchange Brewery Tavern. Both premises were converted to temporary office accommodation in 1946 by Doncaster Corporation.

Cleveland Street at the Young Street junction, with premises on the latter thoroughfare awaiting demolition. The commercial premises featured on Young Street include those once belonging to A. Brown (estate agent), Tom Jaques (electrical store), E. Robinson (fruit and provisions), G. Smith (draper).

A new subway under construction beneath Trafford Way to link the Arndale (now French Gate) Centre to the railway station. On the left is the Grand Theatre whilst Edwards Motor Co. is to the right.

Clearance in French Gate and St Sepulchre Gate prior to the construction of the Arndale Centre. The Guild Hall in French Gate dominates the centre of the picture.

Work on the Golden Acres site is under way with the old Spring Gardens thoroughfare running across the centre of the picture. In the distance, part of the old Turf Tavern can be seen on St James' Street.

View from Bowers Fold looking at new structures being erected in Duke Street during the mid-1960s.

Littlewoods store under construction in Baxter Gate.

Rank's (formerly Hanley's) Mill pictured before clearance.

View taken near Balby Bridge, looking towards the town centre, showing new housing developments.

Northern bus station under construction 23 October 1966.

Both pictures show property clearance along Spring Gardens during the early 1960s. Former England football manager, Kevin Keegan once lived on Spring Gardens.